JEANNE BEKER

THE BIG NIGHT OUT

ILLUSTRATED BY
NATHALIE DION

TUNDRA BOOKS

Published in Canada by Tundra Books,
481 University Avenue, Toronto, Ontario M5G 2E9

Published in the United States by Tundra Books of Northern New York,
P.O. Box 1030, Plattsburgh, New York 12901

Library of Congress Control Number: 2004110126

Library and Archives Canada Cataloguing in Publication

Beker, Jeanne
   The big night out / Jeanne Beker ; Nathalie Dion, illustrator.

ISBN 0-88776-719-2

   1. Rites and ceremonies – Juvenile literature. 2. Parties – Juvenile
literature. 3. Etiquette for young adults. 4. Beauty, Personal.
I. Dion, Nathalie II. Title.

GV1472.B443 2005   j646.7   C2004-904122-3

We acknowledge the financial support of the Government of Canada through the
Book Publishing Industry Development Program (BPIDP) and that of the
Government of Ontario through the Ontario Media Development Corporation's
Ontario Book Initiative.

We further acknowledge the support of the Canada Council for the Arts and
the Ontario Arts Council for our publishing program.

Design: Terri Nimmo

Printed in Canada

1 2 3 4 5 6   10 09 08 07 06 05

To Bekky and Joey, my precious two originals

J.B.

*To all the young girls who might approach fashion
too seriously. May this lighten your "big night out"
and make it a playful experience.*

N.D.

CONTENTS

the BIG
NIGHT
OUT

being an original

The importance of making your own statement . . .

When I was a very little girl, I had this fantasy about going to a big fancy ball in a Viennese palace. I'd picture the scene so often and so perfectly in my mind's eye that I could actually hear the music – Strauss waltzes, to be exact. There I was, wearing an exquisite satin ball gown, in the arms of some handsome European count, being expertly twirled around a big marble dance floor. Above us, a giant crystal chandelier sparkled like a galaxy of brilliant stars. I was dizzy with happiness as I glided across that ballroom with my mysterious foreign count, proud as punch to be feeling so utterly beautiful. I was sure that, one day, I'd grow up to realize my dream.

By the time I was nine, I got to go to my first big dress-up affair: my sister

> "I like to stand out and be myself rather than look like everyone else . . . if you follow everyone else's style, you will never know your true self!"
>
> RACHIE, AGE 12

Marilyn's Sweet Sixteen party. My mother's Italian dressmaker whipped up an amazing original creation for me. It was a pouffy pink organza number that made me look like a human cupcake. With my skinny, white kneesocked legs sticking out of that humongous tulle crinoline, I felt a tad geeky at first. But by the time my mom's hairdresser – who insisted that I looked like my favorite movie star, Audrey Hepburn – did my long brown hair up in an elegant bun, the magic took flight. I suddenly felt very poised and rather perfect. It was the first time I became aware of how a pretty dress and a fancy hairdo could actually transform you.

My first real "big night out" was when I was thirteen. A really cute guy named Sammie asked me to be his date to a Bar

Mitzvah. A group of our classmates were going together, and I was determined to "stand out" in something special. My mother was making a lot of our clothes back in those days, so we went downtown to a fabric store called Stitsky's. Together we chose some lovely magenta lace fabric, which she masterfully turned into an empire-style gown with a scoop neck and puffy little sleeves. I felt terribly grown-up in that dress – rather divine, and quite like a princess. A pair of silver pumps completed my look. I'm sure Sammie was impressed, even though we were all still too shy to dance.

I didn't mastermind my next big party dress until my own Sweet Sixteen.

the magazine picture was that those "booties" were really just sparkly kneesocks. But our poor dear dressmaker struggled with the unstretchy fabric nonetheless, and managed to make me booties, with zippers up the front. Of course, I couldn't slide around in mere fabric on my feet, so I found a pair of extra large turquoise patent shoes – three sizes larger than what I'd normally wear! I managed to squeeze into them with my booties – definitely not the most comfortable footwear for boogying on the dance floor, but they sure did look great! I also sported three pairs of

By then, I was a bit of a wild child. It was the swinging '60s, and I was a wannabe pop diva – very theatrical, and adamant about being a true original. My mother recruited a German dressmaker to help me realize my fantasy outfit. I got the idea from the 1967 holiday edition of *Harper's Bazaar* magazine: a sparkly, long-sleeved, skintight aqua mini dress with matching booties. The dressmaker went to work with this fabulous fabric my mom and I had found on sale. The only trouble was, the fabric didn't have any stretch to it. The dressmaker had to sew zippers up the sleeves in order for them to be so skintight. And what I didn't realize from

Q Dear Jeanne:
I've had my eye on a great pair of shoes to wear to my prom. I told my friend about them, and that I was thinking of getting them. And now she went out and bought them herself! I'm so upset. What should I do?

Shoeless

A Dear Shoeless:
While it may have been insensitive of your friend to have "scooped" you on the shoes, you should feel flattered that she admires your taste so much. If you can't find another pair that you like as much, I'd just buy the same pair and make sure you let her know how happy you were to be of service to her in discovering them in the first place.

Q

Dear Jeanne:
I love my best friend, but she never seems to have any confidence in choosing things for herself, and always tries to copy my style. Should I tell her I don't like this copycat behavior?
The One and Only Me!

A

Dear One and Only:
I think you have to try and encourage your friend to develop her own sense of style. Try praising any unique style traits she might display. Let her know, in a nice way, that you work really hard at being an original, and perhaps you could help her find her own fashion voice. If she still insists on copying you, just feel proud that you're a trendsetting leader and not a mere follower.

nominated as queen of my high school prom. I longed to wear something really unusual, so I had my mom make me an "I Dream of Jeannie" outfit. *I Dream of Jeannie* was a popular TV show at the time about a beautiful female genie who lived in a bottle and always wore a sexy harem outfit. I thought the look would be fun and fitting for my prom, where most of the girls were going to wear conventional, boring gowns. I picked a banana yellow, silk fabric for the jumpsuit part, with black velvet and gold sequin trim for the little bolero vest. Teamed with a pair of crystal-beaded sandals, my harem outfit was a knockout, and really turned heads. Unfortunately, though, I didn't win the "queen of the prom" title. That went to a beautiful popular girl, ironically named Gina. She wore a burgundy gown – very

false eyelashes (two on the top, one on the bottom), a round, shiny, silver face "decal" on my cheek, which was a kind of sticker that I bought at a groovy boutique, and a pair of humongous, turquoise, dangling plastic ball earrings. I put my ultra-long hair up in two high ponytails on either side of my head, and a true dancing queen was born. It was one of the best nights of my life.

The next year, I was

expensive-looking, but quite ordinary. So even though I didn't make it as "queen," I still felt special. Besides, that crown would have looked stupid with my harem outfit, I reasoned.

Looking back, it seems that being "an original" may have been a little easier in those days: Getting clothes custom-made wasn't that uncommon because there were lots of good European dressmakers around who didn't charge an arm and a leg. And mothers had way more time back then, so for those of us lucky enough to have moms who knew how to sew, it was like having your own in-house couturiere. We also weren't as bombarded with so many images of fashion. When I was a kid, great fashion seemed to exist only in the pages of glossy magazines. Today, it's everywhere: TV is flooded with all kinds of fashion, and designers have become household names. Besides getting to see all the international runway collections on television almost as soon as they're staged, we also get to meet the designers and hear directly what they had in mind when they were creating their collections.

MANDY MOORE

"When I'm casual, I'm completely jeans, T-shirt, flip-flops. . . . So when I dress up and I'm going to that other extreme, I want to be feminine, I want to be comfortable, and not be 'too much' I guess."

But beyond all those fashion programs on TV, we're also getting a big fix of fashion through channels like MuchMusic and MTV. Music videos are the perfect platform for stylish pop stars to "express themselves," and in the process, they start trends that we all scramble to copy. From haircuts to the way jeans are cut, TV plays a major role in shaping our concepts of style and what ultimately appeals to us.

And then there are all those "red-carpet" pre-award shows, where we get to see our favorite stars glammed-up to the max, and actually hear them go on about their fabulous outfits. So with all that information and imagery bombarding us, it's hard to hold on to our own unique ideas, and difficult not to be greatly influenced by what we see.

15

finding your style

While everybody seems to be much more fashion savvy these days, many are still quite content to "follow the leader" when it comes to getting dressed. While there's nothing wrong with being conventional and not wanting to particularly stand out from the crowd, coming up with your own ideas about how you want to look – especially for your first, big night out – is not only fun and exciting, but satisfying too. In the fashion world, creativity is the most celebrated thing. And while everyone can't have the genius of a Karl Lagerfeld (who designs for Chanel) or a John Galliano (who designs for Dior), there's no question that if you enjoy fashion, you should be encouraged to come up with exciting new ways to strut it. All it takes is a little imagination, and a little nerve.

No matter how much we might admire the look and style of any one of our particular icons out there, trust me: Most of them don't really put their outfits together themselves. As a matter of fact, most of them don't even shop themselves! These days, all the big stars have professional stylists to do it for them – talented, creative men and women who are fashion experts that often travel the world in search of just the right dress, or pair of shoes, or piece of jewelry for their clients. These trusted stylists sometimes get paid a thousand dollars a day for their services! And the best ones are in high demand. When they choose a fabulous outfit for the star they're dressing, and all the critics approve, the stylist is in heaven. But, sometimes, the poor stylist makes a bad choice, and the star has a very hard time living down all the bad press. So

17

Q

Dear Jeanne:
I know those belly-revealing looks are really in right now, but I've still got some baby fat, and don't feel right about exposing my midriff.
Any suggestions?

Baby Fat

A

Dear Baby:
Don't ever do something you don't feel right about – especially when it comes to style. Surely, there are enough flattering options out there for all our different body shapes and sizes. Never be a fashion victim! Sometimes, it's best not to play up the bits of our bodies that we're self-conscious about. Make up for it in another way and play up your best features instead.

despite the good or bad reviews, one thing's for certain: Everyone – even the big successful superstars – has to take a chance sometimes, and do something a wee bit scary. And in the world of style, that means stepping out of the image we have of ourselves once in a while, and trying something a little different. Otherwise, we get stuck in the same headspace forever. We never change. We never grow. We never evolve into the exciting, inspiring people we all have the potential to be.

Before you're ready to start experimenting – or even shopping, for that matter – you have to examine yourself, and try to discover what kind of style statement you'd really like to make, what you'd like to communicate about yourself (since clothes are such a great means of communication), and who your "style self" really is. By "style self," I mean the part of yourself that's really excited by fashion, that gets turned on by color and romance and beauty, that has particular dreams and fantasies – ways of seeing the world, and your place in it.

First and foremost, looking good is about feeling good. Without question, feeling good on the inside comes first: If you don't like who you are, you'll have a hard time liking the image you're projecting to the public. But once you've learned to like yourself, and feel good about how hard you try to be the best possible person you can be each and every day, once you've accepted things about yourself that may not be within your power to change, you need to start working on liking and appreciating that image you see in the mirror.

Let's start with something simple: Color. We've all had a favorite color for as long as we can remember, right? For some of us, color can become a kind of signature, since we always tend to choose things in a particular shade or two. Soon, people begin associating us

with these certain colors. But while a special color may appeal to us for various reasons, not every color might look great on us. Run around your home and find ten pieces of clothing in different colors. These clothes don't have to fit you – you're only going to have them there to do a test. Look in the mirror and hold up each garment to your face, one at a time. Now be honest. *What colors look best?* There's no question that certain colors just suit some people better than others. So even though you may adore green, and long to live your life surrounded by green things, some shades of green may just not let you look your best, and you might want to avoid wearing them. Look at yourself carefully. Take into account the color of your eyes, your hair, and your skin. But the bottom line is wearing what *you* think you look good in. Because if you *don't* like what you see in the mirror, you won't feel good about yourself. And if you don't

feel good about yourself, it's hard to look good.

The next thing you might want to think about is shape. That's something that's totally up to you, of course, and most of it has to do with comfort. How comfortable will you be – both physically and mentally – in a *big* party dress? By that, I mean one that has a huge skirt, or immense sleeves, or one that's ultra long. Some girls feel very special in these gigantic "serious" gowns. But it takes a lot of personal confidence to pull something like that off, and, quite frankly, all that extra fabric could weigh you down. After all, nothing's better than feeling free and unrestricted. Still, the decision is up to you about how big and cumbersome a dress you want to go for.

"I admire no one's style. I like to mix and match different styles."

RILEY, AGE 14

19

The shape of your body might also dictate what type of dress you choose, and which fabrics you should or shouldn't consider. Some fabrics just aren't that flattering on certain body types. For example, if you're on the large side, a big bold print on a flimsy fabric could make you look even larger. If you don't mind, then that's cool. But if you're self-conscious about your size, you might want to go with a delicate print, or a solid color, in a fabric that isn't too clingy. You might also consider wearing a bra-friendly dress, so you can get the support you need. If you're petite, and want to look taller, a long fitted dress in a solid color would be your best bet. A full-length ruf-fle, which runs from your neck all the way down, would also create the illusion of height. You might want to avoid an especially full skirt, which could overpower you. On the other hand, if you're tall and slim, you might want to wear a full skirt, which would be flattering for your small butt and hips. A pretty belt around your midsection might also help define your waist a bit more.

There are all kinds of factors to consider when it comes to choosing fabric. Some are just too plain heavy for warmer times of the year. Some wrinkle too easily. Some are too delicate, and might snag. Some stain more easily than others. Imagine spilling something on your dress in the middle of your big night out, trying to wash the stain out with water, and then having the water stain your dress! It's happened to me, with very high quality silks. Not a pretty picture. Then there are those fabrics that just feel

Q

Dear Jeanne:
My parents have given me a curfew that's really unfair. How can I get them to give me a later time, like my friends?
Cheated

A

Dear Cheated:
The only thing you can do is to talk reasonably and maturely to your parents, and try to find out why they have a problem with you coming home just a bit later on this most special night. You could start by showing them just how responsible you are. Really work on that. Unfortunately, though, sometimes it's hard to change a parent's mind. You might have them talk to some of your friends' parents. It can be a pretty scary world out there sometimes, and parents often feel a little overprotective. Be thrilled with the knowledge that they love and care about you so much. Perhaps they'd let you host a small sleepover for some of your friends after your "big night." That way, you'd all have the same curfew.

clothes can say so much about you, you'll want to make sure that your outfit really reflects who you are. *Charming and demure? Offbeat and lively? Mysterious and exotic? Flamboyant and funky? Moody and unpredictable?* There are all kinds of messages you can convey with the clothing you choose – just make sure you're true to yourself.

You also might want to think about piecing your outfit together with a number of different elements, rather than going with a one-piece dress. We'll explore some possibilities a little later in the book. For now, just try and imagine what you think would best suit you. While this special big night out is unquestionably meaningful for all your friends, it's a memory that will stick with you for the rest of your life. Make it matter. Try not to be too influenced by what your friends are going to be wearing. Make your own voice heard. You are a true original, after all, with your own unique way of looking at the world and your own unique style. Try not to compromise your precious individuality, and your own vital spirit. This is your night to shine! Make the most of it.

too stiff, and the ones that are too transparent (and demand you wear a slip). But the worst in my mind are the fabrics that are itchy. I'd strongly suggest avoiding them, unless you're intent on inventing a new dance-step called The Scratch.

The image you want to project is another big consideration. Because

21

looking for inspiration

Sparking your creativity and dealing with copycats!

While you may already have a great idea of just the way you want to dress for your first big night out, it's always good to try and keep an open mind. Depending on how long you have to prepare for this special occasion, you might want to do a little research and find out what all the possibilities are before you commit yourself to a certain look. Of course, fashion magazines are the most likely place to start, and the wide array of magazines out there can be dizzying! Spend a little time poring over a number of your favorites, and cut out pictures of looks that really appeal to you. After a while, you're likely to see certain trends appearing. Just for fun, sketch your own fantasy creation. See if any of the dresses in the magazines come close.

You might also want to look at some of the entertainment magazines, and see what your favorite celebrities are wearing. But whatever you do, remember this: Hours and hours go into making these models and stars look this perfect. And there are teams of experts on hand to ensure that every little hair on their heads is picture perfect. And sometimes, there's more to it than that: Often, photos are tweaked digitally, or airbrushed. So some of what you're seeing isn't real at all! That's why it is foolish to ever compare yourself to any of these models or stars. Like it or not, the fashion business is largely based on illusion – creating beauty that could

never realistically exist. So take these fabulous images you see with a grain of salt, and know that real people in real life don't normally look very much like what you're seeing on the pages of these magazines. Still, theses images do provide great fantasies and, sometimes, great inspiration.

If you've got the time, it might also be a good idea to go window-shopping, which is always fun . . . and inexpensive! Window-shopping will give you an idea of which stores you'd like to visit once you do begin your shopping spree. And you'll be able to spend time checking out a variety of looks at your leisure. Take your mom, an aunt, your sister, or a friend with you, so you're able to discuss some of the options you're seeing. Sometimes, expressing your opinions and listening to someone else's helps you to understand why you do or don't like a certain look.

There's no question that all your friends will have a lot to say about what they think you should, or shouldn't, be wearing. Just remember that, when it comes to fashion, there are no real right or wrong answers. Style is a very subjective thing – that means that it's different for everybody and, ideally, should be. While there are certainly lots of girls out there who may enjoy playing follow the leader – because they feel it's safe and easier than thinking for themselves – there are usually very few rewards in copying someone else's style. First of all, it won't likely give you a sense of satisfaction to just pick up on someone else's ideas. Secondly, some girls don't enjoy being copied, and could hold it against you. But if you feel that there's someone who is copying you, please don't get angry with her. If anything, you

should feel sorry for her, that she doesn't have the courage and confidence to think for herself. In a way, you should be flattered that she thinks so highly of your ideas. But, at the end of the day, remember that even though your friends may try to wear the same thing that you do, everybody truly struts style differently.

One time, a group of very fashionable, high profile Toronto ladies who happened to own the same designer suit decided to prove that it didn't really matter if everyone showed up in the same outfit because true style shines uniquely from within. We all agreed to meet for lunch at a very upscale restaurant, dressed in these identical suits. Everybody in the restaurant turned to stare at us as we all sat there smugly. And everyone was amused . . . especially us! Even though we were all wearing the same chic outfit, our accessories were all different, and each one of us truly exuded our own individual style. It was an interesting exercise, and certainly taught me not to fret if someone shows up somewhere wearing the same thing as I am. It should be looked upon as a celebration – a tribute to our own good taste!

I do remember one time, though, when I was a little girl, that my older sister Marilyn had to go shopping for a fancy dress to wear to her grade eight graduation. Marilyn was a very smart

Q

Dear Jeanne:
I really want to wear pants to my friend's Bat Mitzvah party, but my mom says she doesn't think that's proper. Do you?

Slacking Off

A

Dear Slacking Off:
These days, I don't think many of the old fashion rules apply. I'm sure your mother is just thinking a little more conventionally about what most of the other girls will be wearing. It's hard to think of "pants" as being as fancy as a skirt or dress. Still, I think the right dressy pants, made out of the right fabric, with the right cut, could be fabulous. What about a pair of satin palazzo pants? Or a beautiful pair of velvet evening trousers? Just because you're in pants doesn't mean you can't dress up your look with fantastic accessories. But as much as we all adore fashion, I don't think it's ever worth fighting about.

girl, a bit of a bookworm really, but not particularly fashionable. And she wasn't at all popular yet, either. She was what we call a late bloomer. Feeling a little socially awkward, she really had no idea about the kind of dress to wear. So our whole family went out with her, scouring the stores for just the right dress that was both pretty and affordable. After

MARY-KATE OLSEN

"Just do whatever makes you feel most comfortable – not just [what's] in fashion. Don't let anyone tell you that you can't do something, or be something that you want to."

Q

Dear Jeanne:
I'll be going to my school formal with a group of kids. But some of them have boyfriends, and I think their boyfriends are going to buy them corsages. My dad offered to get me a corsage, but I'm not sure that's right. What do you think?

Rosie

A

Dear Rosie:
I certainly don't see anything wrong with a proud and loving father giving his beautiful daughter a corsage to wear to her school formal. You might find it a little awkward to explain just who your "secret admirer" is. And you could go two ways: Keep everybody guessing, or tell them it was a gift from the most special man in your life – your dad!

hours and hours of looking, we found the perfect one: a lovely chiffon dress, with a big flare skirt, trapeze back, and large pink flowers. Even though Marilyn's favorite color had always been blue – and blue truly did look best on her – we all decided this pink-flowered dress was rather spectacular, and Marilyn had to have it.

The night of the big graduation party, the family watched as Marilyn transformed into a regular Cinderella: She felt so glamorous and special in her fabulous new dress. We all proudly accompanied her to the graduation ceremony, but just as the students were lining up to collect their diplomas, we saw a sickening sight: Another girl had the same dress on as Marilyn, except hers had beautiful blue flowers on it – the color we all knew Marilyn would have preferred! My heart sank as I took a good look at the other girl. She was a very popular girl named Muriel, who all the guys liked. Muriel was very well endowed, rather stunning, and oozed confidence – not like our waifish, bespectacled Marilyn, who was lovely in her own way but a bit of a wallflower. Afterwards, at the grad dance, I stood in a corner and watched everybody flock around the babe-acious Muriel as Marilyn simply stood on the sidelines, no doubt feeling a little overwhelmed. I know it shouldn't have mattered, but I felt wretched about it. Today, with all that I know, I realize I shouldn't have felt bad for Marilyn. She grew up determined to have a wonderful, offbeat, unique sense of style, and even today, always goes the extra distance when it comes to choosing unusual accessories that help give her an extraordinary edge. After the graduation-dress experience, I think we all realized the value in wearing original creations. And it was shortly thereafter that my mom invested in her sewing machine. My sister and I had an amazing one-of-a-kind wardrobe from then on. But, ironically, for us, store-bought clothing would still always hold an exotic appeal.

Be adventurous! That's the best advice I could give to anyone looking for inspiration in any aspect of his or her life. We've all spent so long looking in mirrors that, sometimes, we get locked into a certain way of seeing ourselves. We become creatures of habit, especially in the wardrobe department. It becomes much easier to keep going back to the same colors, same styles, same brands and labels, than to try something new. But, as I said earlier, unless we're willing to experiment, we'll never grow. Exposing our-selves to as much fashion as possible is our best bet: We've got to be able to see all the options out there before we can know what's really right for us.

But that doesn't mean just referring to conventional fashion magazines, or shopping the stores, or watching fashion on TV. People-watching can provide great inspiration. Imagine the city sidewalks as the world's largest runway. That's one of my favorite pastimes when I sit in Paris cafés: I simply watch all the different people go by, and take note of each one's unique way of putting themselves together. Of course, some do it better than others. But it really is fun to imagine how the person you see before you got dressed and to try to understand why he or she chose to wear what they did. Streets all over the world are brimming with great inspiration. As a matter of fact, most of the world's top designers have all told me that their main inspiration usually comes from the street. Nothing like a little reality to make our fantasies take flight!

the shopping experience

A practical approach to buying stuff . . .

Now that you've done your research, and are informed and inspired, let the adventure begin! While it's not always possible, it's best to have some time on your side. Don't ever leave your shopping to the last minute because all that pressure is bound to take the fun out of the experience.

The first thing you have to do is set a budget for yourself. Whether your parents are going to generously pay for your purchases, or you plan on dipping into your own savings, you have to know before you step into that retail wilderness just how much you're prepared to spend for your big night out. This is when reality rears its head. But remember this: Great style has little to do with money.

I know that we all often drool over fabulous, expensive clothing. And the international best-dressed lists seem to be ruled by the mega rich. But a little "priceless" imagination often goes a long way in helping achieve memorable, original style. I've spent the past twenty years schmoozing and socializing with some of the wealthiest, most fashionable world travelers around – people who really have the opportunity to get out there and spend, spend, spend. But just because they wear all the "right" labels doesn't make them seriously stylish. What matters most is their winning personalities and insightful souls. If they aren't great people to begin with, all those fancy clothes wear thin very shortly.

I've also had the opportunity to meet some of the world's most creative and inspiring people. And it's always their warm hearts and generous spirits that shine far beyond the clothes they wear. As matter of fact, the most stylish people I've met had such interesting and imaginative

29

"We try not to pay attention to the negative things because that will just make you crazy and make you worry too much about what other people think of you. But as long as we're comfortable with what we're doing – what we're representing – then it's okay."

ways of putting their looks together, and ways of strutting it with such confidence and ease, that they made me realize true style has little to do with how much one spends on their wardrobe. Nevertheless, there are times in life that might call for a little shopping spree . . . no matter what kind of budget you have to work with. Here are some things to take into consideration:

1 What is the maximum amount you have to spend? This should be a figure that will cover your entire look, including shoes, bag, hose, and other accessories.

If you require special lingerie (like a slip, a crinoline, a cammy, or a strapless bra), you might have to consider that as well. It may also include the services of a hairdresser, if you're not planning to do your hair yourself, or maybe even a manicurist. You might also need to buy some new makeup, like a specific color of lipstick or eye shadow.

2 Taking all the different elements of your "look" into consideration, how much of your budget do you want to devote to your actual dress? Or, if it's a series of pieces that will comprise your outfit, make sure you leave enough for each individual one. You might also want to take a long hard look at your existing wardrobe, and see if there are any elements that you might consider using. For example, you might already have a wonderful little top that you could pump new life into by teaming it with a fabulous new skirt. Or maybe you've already got an amazing pair of shoes that are just begging to be partnered with the right new dress. It's a very cool concept to make use of some of the things you already have, and not be extravagant when it comes to acquiring new ones just for the sake of having them. You could even get especially creative and crafty, and think about making changes to some of the existing pieces in your wardrobe. Decorating a simple T-shirt

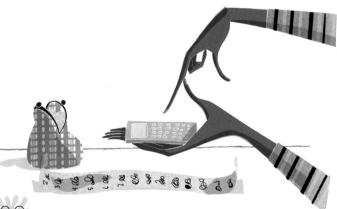

with embroidery, ribbons, beads, or sequins, for example, is an inexpensive way to create an original garment that will help you make an extra special personal style statement, happily leaving you with more to spend on other elements of your outfit.

3 Make a list of all the shops you want to hit. If you're not sure which places might be appropriate to check out, don't be afraid to ask around. Seek out those people whose sense of style you admire, and find out where they shop. It's unlikely that all the shops you'll want to visit will be in the same part of town, so you may

have to extend your shopping spree over a few days. Actually, it's best not to try and get it all done in one day. Take time to savor each one of your purchases, without being overwhelmed by too much running around and spending too much money. Give yourself time to formulate new ideas, without getting everything on impulse.

4 Check out alternative stores for inspiration. Even though vintage may not be your preference, there's no question that many of these nostalgic looks are influencing fashion in major ways these days. It's also very cool to mix vintage pieces with new ones, or just wear vintage accessories to accent your look. Lots of Hollywood celebrities have been popularizing this trend, and many of them have achieved memorable, highly original looks as a result. Besides, vintage clothing is usually a lot more affordable. Aside from vintage specialty shops, you might also want to do some scouting around at various thrift stores. These "secondhand" Goodwill-type shops can be real treasure troves, and you never know what kind of precious piece you might find at a real bargain price. In fact, one quirky accessory might inspire a whole outfit!

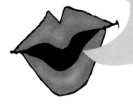

"If you are creative and take some time to think about it, you don't have to spend a fortune to look great."

STEPHANIE, AGE 11

The best part of this type of shopping is that it's highly unlikely that anyone else will show up wearing the same thing.

5 How much use will you be getting out of your purchases? Obviously, it's best to try and maximize the potential use of anything you're planning to buy. That way, spending a little more on a particular item will make more sense. With each thing you plan to purchase, ask yourself about its practicality. *Is this one big night the only time you'll be able to wear the dress, the shoes, or the various accessories?* If you can think of more events coming up in the future (the not-too-distant future, mind you, because you're likely to outgrow some of these things) for which you'll be able to wear elements from your special outfit, then spending a little more won't be as painful or seem as extravagant.

6 Make sure you plan to shop with someone whose opinion you really value. It might be your best friend, your mother, your aunt or sister . . . even your brother or dad (if they have the interest, and the patience!). Shopping alone isn't necessarily the best or most enjoyable way to go, since you won't have anyone to bounce things off. I also wouldn't advise serious shopping

with a whole gang of friends – too many opinions at once might only confuse you. However, if you're pretty confident in the style department, you might want to go browsing on your own, with your parents' permission, of course. That way you can do more research, and then bring a friend or trusted advisor by before you dole out the dough.

7 If your parents are footing the bill for your spree, you really do have to take what they say into consideration. But make sure you have them listen to your point of view, too. Explain to them that you've done your research, and have very strong ideas about how you'd like to look for your big night. They may not agree with your concept, but there are undoubtedly ways you might be able to compromise. Luckily for my teenaged daughters, I've always believed in freedom of expression when it comes to fashion. Granted, I'd probably freak out if they wanted to get tattooed, or piercings in places I thought were inappropriate, but I believe a little innocent fun in the dress-up department is healthy. Your parents might have other ideas, of course. All you can do is plead your case intelligently, calmly, responsibly, and try to make them understand that you need and appreciate their support. Maybe you can all find a reasonable compromise. Most parents just want

Q Dear Jeanne:
I've fallen in love with this fabulous dress, but it's really low cut. How low is too low? I don't want to look trampy. But I do think the dress is gorgeous. Help!
Cleo

A Dear Cleo:
Comfort is key. You want to be able to feel great about what you're wearing – not self-conscious. And remember, it's not the clothes that have to be gorgeous, but how you look in them that counts. Think about how old you are and whether this vampy look is really appropriate for someone your age. And ask your parents' opinion. While you might not always agree with what they have to say, their opinions are usually based on life experience, and that really does count for a lot.

their kids to be happy, and they want to protect them from making stupid mistakes. Know they love you – and maybe they'll be able to learn something from you, just as you learn so many things from them. Mutual respect is key.

8 Now have a good breakfast (or lunch), put on some comfortable shoes, and let the shopping begin!

● ● ● ● ● ●

Q Dear Jeanne:
I'm a very athletic person, and while I know I'm in good shape, I think I might look a little stocky. Any suggestions for a dress that would flatter me?

Tough but Toned

A Dear Toned:
Go for something feminine, like a dress with ruffles, or perhaps a slit, or a tulle or chiffon skirt to soften your image. A halter dress, or something strapless, will show off your nicely toned arms. A chiffon scarf would be just the thing to wrap around your shoulders, and add an air of grace and femininity to your look.

Whether or not you have an adult accompanying you on your shopping spree, you must be in control when it comes to dealing with the sales staff. As the consumer – the one who's going to be spending the money – you have certain rights. Sometimes, salespeople take advantage of younger consumers who may not be that sure of what they want. These overeager salespeople may try talking you into purchases that you're really not crazy about, or that aren't appropriate for you. Or, they may not take you seriously, not realizing that you are indeed on an important mission and do intend to buy something,

if the right thing appears. If a salesperson is rude to you, politely ask to speak to the store manager. Wise shop owners appreciate their customers, and if you don't feel you're getting the respect you deserve, take your business elsewhere. We live in a very competitive retail environment, and shops can't afford to treat customers with disrespect.

Before you ask for help, you might want to scour the racks on your own, just to suss out what each particular store has to offer, and whether you feel it's right for you. When it comes to choosing garments to try on, it's imperative that you ask for a salesperson's help in finding the right size. If you're looking for something in particular that you just can't find, don't be afraid to ask for help. Sometimes, there are wonderful items that have been put aside for some reason, or maybe there are other great pieces that you've accidentally overlooked. A kind and courteous

salesperson will be only too happy to lend a hand.

While many of these experienced sales staff are often good judges of what looks best on people, in the end, what to buy has to be your decision. Not only should the item fit properly – unless it's possible to get it altered – but it must feel right. You should like what you see in that mirror. Don't let anybody talk you into anything you're not sure about. If the store has a return policy, all the better. That will give you a chance to take the item home and really make sure that it's right for you. Otherwise, you could get stuck with something inappropriate, that you've bought impulsively.

If you see the perfect dress, and it's not available in your size, ask if the store has other branches they can check. Or, if there's enough time, try to contact the manufacturer of the dress to see if any other shops in the area are carrying it in your size. You might also consider using an alterationist. Sometimes, the shop will do the alterations for you, at no cost. Other times, there's a minimal cost. But if an alterationist isn't available through the shop, you may have to seek one out on your own. Otherwise, you'll be stuck with an ill-fitting garment.

Even though you may start your shopping spree looking for a great dress, or other type of outfit, if you see an incredible pair of shoes that really speak to you, you might want to consider buying them first, and building your look around them. These days, accessories often play starring roles in the outfit department, and because great accessories can really make an outfit, I see nothing wrong with starting with your feet first. Remember: In fashion, there are no rules.

Hopefully, you'll have more than one day to do your shopping. You're going to need time to digest all those fabulous clothes and accessories you're seeing. And there's something wonderful about really savoring each and every purchase. So while you may be tempted to "go nuts" and assemble your special outfit in one fell swoop, try to restrain yourself. Shopping frenzies usually result in shopping mistakes, and with your limited budget, you can't really afford to make any.

the vintage vibe

We're at a point in history where we're becoming especially nostalgic about the past: Things are moving forward quickly, and there's something romantic about looking back and appreciating all the beauty, art, and fashion important to our mothers and grandmothers when they were young. We also live in a society where's there's so much around that's the "same" that we really crave the unique, the unusual, and the unexpected. Maybe that's why vintage dressing has taken off to such a big degree in recent years. If we wear something that's vintage, chances are slim to none that someone else will show up wearing the exact same thing. That's why so many stars have been opting to dress in vintage chic for their red-carpet appearances. From Winona Ryder, to Julia Roberts, to Renée Zellweger, some of the entertainment world's brightest luminaries are hot on the vintage trend, and some have become serious collectors.

Many of the models that I've met are also huge vintage fans: Because they have to try on clothes for a living, many have become very astute about what makes a great garment. And many of them develop great taste in clothing. They also tire of the usual fare out there – the stuff that anyone can buy if they can pay the price. So many of these young

"I love vintage clothing because it's unique, great looking, and . . . a fashion that never dies out!"

RACHIE, AGE 12

37

women scour the secondhand and vintage stores in search of exceptional, affordable pieces. The first time I met Kate Moss, very early in her career, she was wearing an old vintage silk scarf, casually tied around her neck. She was also wearing a teeny little sweater, which looked as though she'd outgrown it, a pair of nondescript old blue jeans, and ratty sneakers. But she exuded a fabulous sense of style. And at least some of it was due to that special scarf, I'm sure!

You may not be interested in dressing in vintage from head to toe. But the odd piece can elevate your outfit to a whole new level. You might go for something as simple as your grandmother's brooch, or maybe an old evening bag that your mom wore in the '60s. You could even pin your vintage brooch on a brand-new evening bag, and create a gorgeous conversation piece. Maybe you could find a pretty little beaded sweater from the '40s, or a capelet from the '30s, or a fabulous circle skirt from the '50s. You'd be especially lucky if you could track down an original flapper dress from the '20s, as that style has come back in a big way. Mixing up clothes from different eras is really fun, and will result in a highly eclectic and original look. But unless you're made of money, you'll want to be cautious in those vintage and thrift shops so you can really suss out the bargains. Because of the popularity of vintage – especially these pieces that are still in good condition – prices have gone through the roof. Some of the garments you find may need a little repair work, so keep that in mind.

1 Examine seams carefully. These are the stress points for any garment. But seams can often be repaired easily.

2 Check out the buttons. While missing buttons can be replaced, chances are pretty slim that you'll be able to find a match. You may have to replace all the buttons, even though just one is missing. But save those vintage buttons that you remove, as many are highly collectable. You might even be able to turn your vintage buttons into interesting pieces of jewelry.

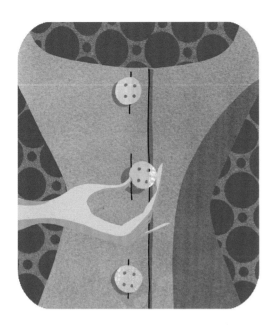

looked does magically surface, and you end up with a bonafide designer garment, which could be valuable indeed.

3 Inspect the garment carefully for stains. While every vintage piece you purchase will no doubt require a good cleaning, many of the stains you see are permanent. Underarm sweat marks are impossible to remove. Makeup stains are also pretty tough, to say nothing about wine, coffee, or tea stains that have been sitting in that garment for years. So if the piece you're eyeing is especially stained, I'd reconsider, unless you plan on dyeing the garment – which could have interesting results.

4 Look for labels. Chances are, any affordable pieces that you'll come across won't sport high-end designer names. Most of those garments will have been snatched up by serious collectors for impossibly high prices. But, sometimes, a fabulous designer piece that got over-

5 Beaded pieces are especially lovely, but if too many of the beads have fallen off, you might have a hard time repairing the work, which was probably done by hand. If just a few beads are missing, it's unlikely anyone will notice, so don't worry.

6 Remember: Vintage fabrics are very old . . . and usually very worn. Chances of tears or little holes (like moth holes) are common. If you find a garment that looks almost pristine, you're in luck! But, otherwise, remember how delicate these old clothes are, especially when you try them on, or begin wearing them. After all, most of the really old fabrics

GWEN STEFANI

*"I always made my own clothes.
I always loved doing that.
I was like a thrift store junkie,
remaking everything."*

don't have any stretch to them. You might even want to carry a needle and thread around with you if purchase something that seems especially delicate, in case you split a seam.

7 The smell of some vintage clothing is a turnoff for some people. While you'll want to make sure these clothes are carefully laundered or dry-cleaned before you

even think of wearing them out, sometimes there may be a faint musty odor that's almost impossible to get rid of. According to vintage-lovers, it's something that you get used to after a while, and eventually, it's not even noticed.

8 Doing some fashion-history research will really enhance your love and appreciation of vintage clothing, and give you a better understanding of where today's designers are getting a lot of their inspiration. You'll become a more fashion-savvy

person, and your taste for fine style and your understanding of trends are bound to improve. Knowing not only what you like, but *why* you like it will be a big help to you – not only now, but later in life too.

● ● ● ● ● ●

You might want to "update" certain vintage pieces that you find by altering them, or adding on to them. A cool label named Imitation of Christ popularized this notion a few years back, "reworking" old vintage clothing and creating highly original, quirky garments that sold for outrageously high prices. Even decorating old vintage T-shirts has become big business for some young designers. There isn't one famous designer I know today who isn't inspired by vintage clothing, or who doesn't appreciate vintage sensibility. Marc Jacobs, one of America's best-loved and most successful young designers, regularly refers to vintage themes in all his popular collections. The whole fashion world believes that we can learn a lot by looking back, as we forge ahead into the future.

Besides vintage stores, thrift shops like Goodwill, and various flea markets and charity bazaars, the Internet also provides great sources for vintage shopping. But shopping on the net has its pros and cons: On the positive side, the world opens up to you, and you can hone in on specific things you might be looking for, or be exposed to things that you would never even think of. But on the downside, you won't have the opportunity try these things on, and because you won't be able to closely examine your finds, there may be some

Q Dear Jeanne:
I'm going to have my first professional manicure, but can't decide what color of polish to get. Should it match my dress exactly, or should I go for something different?

Undecided

A Dear Undecided:
I certainly don't think your nail polish has to match your dress. These days, anything goes! It all depends on how bold a statement you want to make. I do find that if you're going to be wearing red, it's nice to match the same shade of red polish. But nothing looks more elegant than a pale, natural-looking nail – perhaps in an off-white shade, or with a pearlized shimmer. A French manicure is also very chic and classic, and will go well with whatever you decide to wear postprom, even if it's ultra casual.

unexpected surprises, especially if the quality of the piece isn't up to scratch. Still, there *are* some reputable vintage dealers on the web that stand by their merchandise. Just make sure to allow enough time for your purchases to get to you. Shopping on the net may certainly be quicker than conventional boutique-hopping, but you'll have to have patience when it comes to waiting for most deliveries.

winning accents

Accessories galore . . . from shoes to bags to tiaras!

I'm a firm believer that the accessories you choose say a lot about who you are. They can also make or break your outfit, and will inevitably provide you with your strongest "style voice." Accessories can totally transform your look, and help leave lasting impressions. So it's important to put careful thought into the accessories you choose, from your shoes to your bag to your jewelry. A great pair of shoes, or an amazing handbag, or some fabulous jewelry can serve as the focal point of your style statement, and your whole outfit can "revolve" around this particular accessory. It might be something as simple as a terrific belt, or a gorgeous scarf or shawl. These items also serve to update old clothes that you already have, which is especially helpful if you can't really afford to splurge on a whole new outfit.

Let's start with my all-time favorite accessories – and the pièces de résistance of just about every fashion-loving female I know: Shoes. The right pair can transform an outfit, elevate you both physically and psychologically, turn heads and garner great compliments. They can inspire you to walk with grace, and help give you a new air of confidence. The wrong pair, however, can be a nightmare: If the shoes are uncomfortable or poorly designed, they can be difficult to walk in, impossible to dance in, and make you so self-conscious that you can hardly wait to get those suckers off your feet. The wrong shoes can ruin your whole night, unless, of course, you don't mind kicking them off midway through the evening and resorting to bare or stocking feet – which I see young girls doing all the time.

43

If you want to go easy on your tender tootsies right off the bat, you might consider just wearing a pair of chic little ballet slippers, which you could decorate yourself to match your outfit. Some Crazy Glue and sequins could do the trick, or you can get ultra fancy with interesting buttons and bows. Even if you don't want to wear ballerina slippers as your primary footwear, think about bringing a pair along with you if you plan on doing a lot of dancing. They could make the last part of your evening a lot more enjoyable.

When it comes to choosing your dream shoes, just remember the style power they have. Years ago, women often dyed their party shoes to match their dresses. But, nowadays, contrast is fun too. Try to think "out" of the proverbial shoe box, and consider something daring. Purple dress? What about a pair of bright red shoes? Or you could try a funky pair of cowboy boots with your tulle skirt. If there's a Chinatown in your city, you could go looking there for some pretty beaded or embroidered satin slippers, which are exotic and quite affordable. Or you could just resort to your good old Converse sneakers, maybe dressed up with some colored satin ribbon rather than boring old shoelaces, and a few sequins glued on for good measure. That would certainly be an alternative look, teamed with a taffeta party dress. If you're brave and dare to be different, it's a cool and fun look.

"How do you know when shoes are right for you?" I asked famous shoe designer Manolo Blahnik at a recent Dior show in Paris. "A woman just knows," claimed Blahnik, with a twinkle in his eye. "It's a kind of thing you feel in your gut." Wish we all were that in tune with our "guts" because with countless options out there, shoe shopping can be a dizzying experience. Still, for me, it's an experience that's always fun. Unlike shopping for clothes, there are so many types of shoe sizings that if one pair you like doesn't fit right, it's usually not too difficult to find another pair that does.

Shiny patent shoes of any sort are always great for evening. Metallics – like silver, gold, copper, or pewter – are also popular and timeless. And there are some great colorful metallics out there.

Heel height is one of the most important things to consider when choosing shoes. While most females adore the look of a higher heel because of its elegance and the added height it gives, walking on high heels can be a bit of a challenge. If you are thinking about going for a higher heel, make sure you get your shoes with enough time to practice walking in them and to "break them in" a bit. Brand-new shoes can be a little stiff at first, and are often a pain, resulting in blisters and aching feet. Even if you just wear your shoes around your room for a few nights before your big night, it would help tremendously.

Okay . . . back to heel height. A higher heel than you're used to doesn't necessarily mean a stiletto – those ultra-thin, ultra-high heels that are often extremely wobbly. You could go for a little "kitten" heel – a look from the '50s that's come back in a huge way. A kitten heel is very dressy and chic. Or you might consider a chunky heel, which is much more stable for walking, although it might not give you the dainty look you crave. Platforms are pretty comfortable, I find. They certainly give you height, if that's what you're after. Just make sure the platforms aren't too ridiculously high, because they could make you stumble – and a sprained ankle is the last thing you want in the middle of your big night out!

Depending on the season, you might want to choose a pretty sandal. Strappy shoes can look very dressy, but make sure they fit well because nothing's more painful than a too-tight strap. It may stretch out in time, but it could be intolerable for you right off the bat. If you decide to go with open-toed shoes, which can be worn for fancy evening dress year-round, make sure your feet are worthy of showing off! Your toes should be presentable and pretty, and we'll deal with that in the next chapter. Open-toed shoes really do look best when worn with no hose at all, but there are some styles that look interesting with opaque, colored stockings, or textured stockings like fishnets. If you do decide to wear natural hose with your sandals, make sure you're wearing hose with an ultra-sheer toe. While these types of stockings are easier to run, they look so much better. Also, if you're going to be wearing sandals and bare feet, that

would be a good opportunity to sport a pretty toe ring – a little extra bit of glamor to get you through the night.

Fancy hose can be lots of fun, and give your look a whole other dimension. Opaque panty hose in bright, offbeat colors – like hot pink, turquoise, or lime green – can add a lot of pizzazz to an otherwise low-key outfit. Layering hose is cool too: Try a pair of black fishnets over pink hose, or come up with your own interesting color combinations for a really unique look. Lacy hose is particularly pretty too, and an inexpensive way to add some funk and glamor to your ensemble.

If you're going for panty hose, make sure you get the size that's right for you. Nothing's more of a drag than hose that are too short, or too long – very uncomfortable, and you'll feel like you have to pull up your stockings all night long. A lot of girls like stay-up hose. But they do feel a little loose on some girls, and a little tight on others. Again,

buying these things at the last minute can pose problems. Make sure you leave yourself enough time.

Another fun option is fancy little ankle socks – a very hip look that can be both cute and comfortable. Worn with tiny heels, or even a strappy shoe, ankle socks – in just about any color – will inject an edgy, retro feel to your look. Of course, the whole outfit's got to work together. But it's just an alternative to going the conventional "dress up" route.

Great style starts from the inside out: The right lingerie is essential to looking and feeling your best. I'm not suggesting that you run out and buy ultra-expensive, fancy underthings. But you will want to make sure that you've got the appropriate underwear for the outfit you're wearing. Whether it's a strapless bra, panties that won't give you the dreaded panty-line, a camisole if your top is too transparent, or a slip if your skirt is see-through, be sure to deal with all these details well in advance. Nothing like standing in front of the mirror just before you head out and realizing that your bra is all wrong, or you need a good slip. Lovely lingerie is a little luxury that will always make you feel more feminine, and can make a lot of difference to the way your clothes fit.

You'll need a great little bag to pop a few necessary items in for the evening.

couple of quarters for the phone, and money for cab fare if you need to take a taxi. You may also have to carry a ticket to the dance or event you're going to. You might want to pop a tissue or two in your bag as well, and perhaps a small camera. With all those necessary items, a teeny, tiny bag might not be appropriate. Still, it's unlikely you'll want to take one that's cumbersome or awkward to carry.

Of course, evening bags come in all shapes and sizes. Fancy little bags can be expensive, but I wouldn't advise spending too much on this small, yet vital, element of your outfit. This is one place where you can be especially creative. You can get the simplest little pouch, and decorate it with a beautiful brooch for a highly original, personalized look. The same can be done with assorted decorative buttons, all sewn very closely together. That could result in a real conversation piece – certainly an eye-catching accessory that's totally original and inexpensive.

If you're especially crafty and creative, you might want to take an inexpensive lunchbox and really express yourself. Decoupage would be fabulous – cut great pictures out of magazines and make them into a collage to cover your lunchbox. You can also decorate it with fake pearls, gemstones, and ribbons. Or what about artificial flowers? I was recently given a gorgeous little

Perhaps a key, maybe a little compact or mirror, certainly a lipstick or gloss, a comb, a concealer stick perhaps, and maybe a package of gum or some breath mints. If you've got a cell phone but can't fit it in your bag, be sure to take a

straw bag, covered in silk roses. It's romantic and imaginative, and makes a great eye-catching fashion statement. Just ensure you use enough of the right glue so your decorations stick. Nothing like your "designer bag" falling apart in the middle of the dance floor! Actually, you might want to carry a little tube of glue with you, just in case. But if you're not interested in making your own bag, thrift stores usually carry lots of interesting little vintage bags that are attractive and affordable. Or try asking around to see if your mother, your aunt, or any of their friends might have a funky old evening bag you can borrow.

Now for the really yummy part – jewelry! Most of us love our baubles and

beads, and this is the night to really strut our stuff. If you don't like the look of a lot of jewelry, however, that's fine, too. Don't feel obligated to wear it if you want to appear more subdued, but these days, piling it on is quite alright, especially if you like that "glitzy girl" look. At one time, mixing silver and gold together just wasn't done very often. But now, it's a winning combination, so if you feel like indulging, go for it! Pearls are always classically beautiful for evening, and layering on strands can be very chic – like Coco Chanel used to do. You may be an edgier kind of girl, and prefer the tougher look of link chains. Layering chains can look pretty hot too – both around your neck, and on your wrists. Wearing lots and lots of bangles is very cool, and funky big earrings are definitely back. Again, jewelry can really define you, and say a lot about who you are. It certainly doesn't have to be "real," or expensive for that matter. It should only enhance your outfit, and say something about you: Whether it's demure and delicate, brash and sassy, whimsical and fun, or no-nonsense and classic, put a lot of thought into each and every piece you don on your special night.

Maybe you have a piece of jewelry that you're sentimental about: your grandmother's locket, or a little ring your dad gave you, or a special bracelet you got from your best friend. These pieces that have particular meaning usually make us feel good and warmhearted, and are an asset on special occasions because they remind us of those people we love. It's wonderful and quite magical to have these pieces on when we're out celebrating an important event, or just having one of the most memorable nights of our lives. If you've got some special pieces, I urge you to wear at least one of them. They're sure to act as lucky charms, reminding you of how much you're loved, and how unique you really are.

When it comes to earrings, choose ones that are comfortable and not likely to fall off if the dancing gets a little wild. For those of you without pierced ears, you might want to try some clip-ons. But be forewarned: They can feel okay for the first hour or so, but some can be a real "pain in the lobe" by the end of the night! Again, a trial run is always best. Just wear the clip-ons you have in mind the evening before your big night out, and see how comfortable they really are.

Whether or not you wear a watch depends on a few things: If you have one that's dressier than the one you wear every day, you might want to take advantage of this night, and put it on. Obviously, you'll want to wear a watch if you really need to be conscious of the time – and many of you will have to be,

Q

Dear Jeanne:

I've got very hairy arms, and I'm wearing a sleeveless dress to the school formal. Yuck! What should I do?

Monkey Girl

A

Dear Monkey:

If you feel self-conscious about your exposed arms, you might try having your arm hair bleached. Although there are home-bleaching products, this could get to be a rather messy affair. Going to a professional esthetician for bleaching is probably your best bet. You could also have your arms waxed. The hair will come back, but much more sparsely. Whatever you do, don't shave your arms! The hair will grow back very stubbly, and you're sure to regret it. Shaving underarms is quite alright. But NOT forearms, please.

if you're going to be with your friends and have a strict curfew. But you might want to forget a bit about the time on this special night, and not wear your watch for a change. It's really up to you.

Gloves are another great accessory that has made a tremendous comeback, and harkens to a time of true ladylike elegance. Short, delicate white gloves are kind of funky, and you might be able to find some very reasonable ones at a vintage shop. You could even decorate them with sequins or beads to match your outfit. Lacy ones are especially lovely. And if you're wearing a strapless or sleeveless gown, you might think about getting an extra long pair of white or black stretchy evening gloves for a particularly dramatic effect. These extra long gloves are usually kept on all night – even when you're eating. You can wear a fabulous bracelet right over them . . . or even a big honking ring – if you have one that will fit over your gloved finger. Very chic, indeed.

Another important thing to consider is whether or not you'll be needing a little wrap, stole, or sweater to wear over

your outfit. Depending on the time of year, you might need just an overcoat, but if you don't have a "fancy" coat or jacket, you can dress up even the most boring old ski jacket with some fabulous silk flowers, or big glitzy brooches. If the weather's not too chilly, you might just wear a lovely pashmina (the real ones cost a fortune, of course, but there are some gorgeous "fake" ones out there, in sumptuous colors, that aren't expensive at all). For an ultra-glamorous effect, try getting a long piece of chiffon fabric in a color that will complement your outfit, and wrap that around your neck or shoulders. Little cardigan sweaters are always sweet as evening cover-ups, and again, vintage shops often carry beaded ones from the '40s, '50s, and '60s. Or, if you've got the time, you might try sewing some beads on a delicate little sweater that you already have. If the weather's not too hot, you'll probably appreciate having a little wrap or sweater with you, even if you just carry it most of the night, or check it in the cloakroom. You never know how chilly things could get on the way home.

Don't forget to have fun, and get creative with your accessories. If you can't find just the right necklace, try making an unusual choker, with an interesting brooch pinned on to a piece of velvet ribbon simply tied around your neck. Or you could buy several strands of ultra-thin satin ribbon, and tie them all in a beautiful bow at the side of your neck. A big artificial silk flower could look gorgeous pinned to your shoulder – unless, of course, you're going to be wearing a corsage: You wouldn't want the fake flower to compete with the real thing.

And last but not least, I must mention tiaras. They've made an enormous comeback recently, and many fun inexpensive ones are available at some of the

Q

Dear Jeanne:
I'm dying to wear a pair of high heels to my first dance, but the boy I have a crush on is a little shorter than me. I'm worried that he won't ask me to dance if he thinks I'm too tall. What do you think?

Well-Heeled

A

Dear Well-Heeled:
While it's nice that you're being sensitive to your dreamboat's possible insecurities, I wouldn't worry too much. If he's really interested in you, I'm sure he'll ask you to dance no matter how tall you are. Just make sure you let him know YOU are interested in him. And, by the way, why don't you just ask him to dance instead of waiting for the invitation? There are all sorts of high heels out there. If you're nervous about adding height to your stature, just go for a pair that are slightly lower.

funkier clothing boutiques around. Of course, you'll probably be feeling like you're wearing an invisible tiara on this most exciting big night out. But if you do want to get a tad campy, and feel you could pull it off, you might consider wearing an actual rhinestone tiara. Just make sure you do it with a sense of humor – after all, you wouldn't want to be mistaken for the "queen of the prom," would you?

salon state of mind

Hair and makeup tips . . .

Once you've decided on your clothes, shoes, and other accessories, you'll want to hone in on how to wear your hair and makeup to best complement your look. I've been to enough fashion shows to know that the sky's the limit when it comes to hair and makeup. And, honestly, hair and makeup can really make or break a look. I've seen entire runway collections of amazing clothes that have been almost ruined because the models' hair and makeup just weren't right. There's a saying in fashion that "God is in the details." That means that when a lot of attention is paid to the little things, inspired perfection is really achieved. You can be wearing the most exquisite creation, but if your hair's a mess, or done up in a style that doesn't suit you – or if your makeup is too thick and sloppily

applied – you might as well be wearing a potato sack. After all, it's *you* that should be shining: You want people to notice how great *you* look, before they even focus on what you're wearing.

First, *the hair.* If you're happy with the way you wear your hair for every day, and don't want to go to the bother and expense of going to a hairdresser, you might just want to wear it naturally, with a beautiful hair clip or ribbon. That unstructured, natural look is very much in vogue, and even the biggest stars are wearing their hair naturally for their red-carpet appearances. But since it's such a special night, it might be nice to do something a little different. A great hairdo that isn't the one you usually wear is a surefire way of getting attention.

If you always wear your hair down, it might be fun to get an updo for a change. Of course, it would be best to

53

though these irons really dry out your hair if used on a regular basis. At any rate, unless your hair has a lot of body, sometimes these curls won't stay in all night.

It's fun to experiment with different looks – just make sure you start playing around with your hair well in advance of your big night. If you long for curly hair, but aren't sure how it would look, try curling it a few days ahead to see how it takes, and how it looks. Or if you'd like to try straight hair, have it straightened once before your big night to make sure this really is the look you want.

Some of you might be tempted to go

visit a professional hairstylist if you crave something extra fancy. But tying your hair up in a ponytail, if it's long enough, with a fabulous bow around the elastic, could look very hip and happening. Remember, once again, that you want to be comfortable. Sometimes, an elaborate updo that takes dozens of hairpins to keep it in place, with tons of hairspray to hold it up, isn't necessarily that comfortable.

If your hair is curly, you may want to have it blown dry straight for a change. Or you could use a straightening iron, although I don't recommend you make a habit of using one as they can really damage your hair. If your hair is already straight, you might want to add a wave or curl. If it's long, you could just wash it the night before, and braid it. When you take your braids out the next day, you'll have lovely, wavy hair. Or you could set your hair with rollers and setting lotion. Or try a curling iron, for a drastic change on your big night out. I strongly advise against coloring, bleaching, or cutting your hair within a week of your big night. That way, if you aren't happy with the results, you'll have time to make a change. Nothing is worse than getting a bad haircut, or a bad color job, right before you have to look your best. Also, sometimes these changes take getting used to. You may not like the look at first, but in a few days, it "grows" on you. Having your hair altered in advance will give you a chance to be comfortable with your new look, and enable you to strut it with confidence.

There's no question that this would be a fun time to make a change in your appearance, but it doesn't have to be a big permanent change. You might want to try some extensions in your hair. Extensions are fake strands of hair that are glued onto your real hair. They're available in natural hair colors, and fabulous bright colors as well. It's probably best that a professional stylist help attach them for you. But one of my teenaged daughters recently bought some lime green ones that she put into her black hair with the help of a friend, and they looked wonderful. To remove them, you use a special solution that dissolves the glue. Again, I'd advise experimenting with this sort of thing in advance of your big night. Ditto for playing around with

Q Dear Jeanne:
I'd like to go braless, but I'm self-conscious of my nipples. What do you suggest?

Perky

A Dear Perky:
Well, there is a solution, though it might not be your idea of a good time. "Breast Petals" are available – sticky pieces of soft cloth that help conceal your nipples. One company that makes them is Fashion Forms. Not sure how they feel, but, apparently, they work.

any temporary color. Otherwise, you may find yourself on your big night out with pink or purple highlights that you really aren't into.

There are other temporary extensions available – beautifully colored strands that you simply clip into your hair. These could make the most sense, as they can create a dramatic look that you're likely to tire of easily – perfect for your special big night statement.

And don't forget about all the beautiful hair accessories out there to complement your look. From glitzy jeweled hair clips to classy tortoiseshell combs, from attractive "scrunchies" to beautiful headbands, hair accessories can add so much to your 'do, whether you're doing it yourself, or going to a hairdresser.

BETSEY JOHNSON

*"In the old days,
I really had to stick to my guns.
Just going through the '60s and '70s,
I really felt like 'I look so weird!!
How am I gonna keep doing this?!'
But now I'm older, and people
respect older people. When I was
young and looked like this,
they trashed me!"*

Q

Dear Jeanne:
I'm in a wheelchair, and would like to look extra special for my first big dance. Any suggestions, besides the usual dress-up advice?

Wheely Excited

A

Dear Wheely:
Why not make the most of your situation, and dress up your chair as well? It would be fabulous to decorate it with ribbons that match your dress. Or perhaps you could get some silk flowers that complement your outfit, and wrap them around the handles or arms of your chair. I'd pay extra attention to your evening bag as well – get one that really makes a celebratory statement. It could be a wonderful, eye-catching accent to your entire look.

Just make sure any clip or comb you choose holds your hair securely. You don't want to be bothered by a clip that keeps sliding out, or worry all night about losing your lovely hair accessory.

When it comes to *makeup,* very often, less is more – that is to say, the less you use, the more value it will be to you. No one, young or old, looks good in gobs of makeup, unless perhaps they're performing onstage, or walking down a runway. A fresh natural look, with just a hint of color, or perhaps a soft touch of shimmer for evening, is what you should be after. Unless it's a costume party you're going to, you really want to look your best self possible, so don't go overboard with your makeup.

There's so much makeup on the market these days – so many types and brands and colors – that it can really get confusing for "first-time" makeup users. The best thing is to experiment with different types of makeup until you find what's right for you. But since you might not have the time – or money – required to do that, you might want to start by putting together a basic little kit for yourself. I'm not a proponent of using lots of makeup, no matter what your age, but for young teens especially, too much makeup looks cheap, and can ruin your look. You might be satisfied with just a bit of lip gloss, but if you're eager to use a bit more, here's what I suggest:

who usually have those dreaded zits and blemishes to contend with. Some brands manufacture medicated cover-up sticks that may help your zits disappear more quickly.

Blush. Make sure you go really lightly with this. A soft blush with a hint of shimmer can look very pretty, especially on those with pale skin.

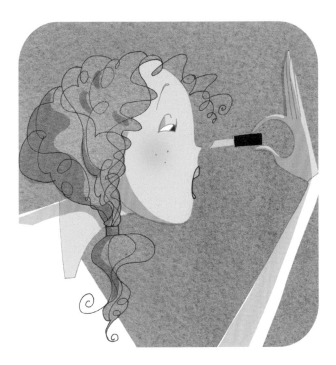

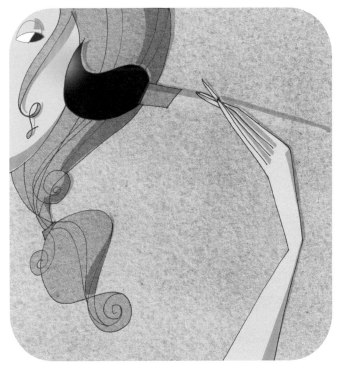

Sheer Lipstick. This should be in a soft color that will complement your dress. Or, if you're wearing bright red, you might want to go with a stronger lip. I do recommend lipstick that's sheer and creamy, though. It might not stay on as long, but it will remain even. You can always reapply throughout the night. For extra dazzle, you can put a sparkly gloss over it.

Cover-up. A concealer stick, in a tone that will blend well with your skin, is a makeup bag staple for young teens,

Eye Shadow. Again, you'll want to go very lightly with anything you put on your eyes. For evening, product with shimmer is always lovely. Try a soft pink or peach or mauve on your lids, and a cream or off-white on the area under your eyebrows.

Eyeliner. You've got to be very careful if you decide to use eyeliner because, if applied poorly, it will give you a cheap and tarty look. Personally, I don't think eyeliner is necessary at all for young teens. But, since my own two teenaged daughters are addicted to the stuff, I understand that it provides a more intense look that some might be after. While you can work with cake eyeliner, or perhaps liquid, and a very fine brush with a very steady hand, maybe it's best to go with a simple eyeliner pencil, in either brown or black, depending on your coloring. But please – go lightly!

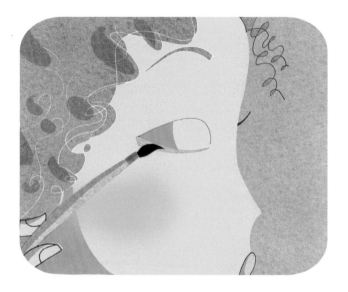

Mascara. We all love our mascara, and if applied gingerly, the effects can be dramatic. Use brown or black, or even a fun color like blue or purple, for a zanier, more colorful look all around. Make sure your mascara is waterproof, to avoid smudging.

Foundation. I'm only including foundation for those of you with problem skin, who might like extra cover-up on your big night. It should be liquid, and water-based, for an extremely light look. It should also be carefully matched to your skin tone by a professional. I see many people trying foundation makeup on their hands. This is wrong, since the color of your hand is usually not the same as that of your face. Anyone working behind the makeup counter should be able to advise you which shade is right for you. Foundation must be blended very carefully. Again, it should be used only if you have too many blemishes to hide with a mere cover stick. And make sure you go with a hypoallergenic brand, just to be safe.

Pressed Powder. A pressed powder compact is a nice addition to any evening bag, mostly because these

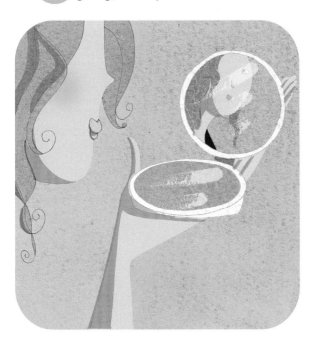

compacts have mirrors in them. Powder isn't necessary for everyone, of course, but those with particularly oily skin might want to take some of the shine off their foreheads, noses, and chins – especially for photos. Again, make sure you get a shade that matches your skin tone.

Face and body glitter is something that we've all been having fun with lately. But don't go overboard: Too much glitter can look cheap and tacky, and ruin any magical effect you might be after. The body lotions with traces of glitter mixed right into them are lovely, and perfect for applying to your arms and chest area if you're wearing something low cut.

Remember: Makeup is meant to enhance our natural beauty. It takes years to perfect the art of applying it, and some people just do it better than others. You have to be patient. And practice really does make perfect: Don't expect to get it right the first time out. Most importantly, keep a light hand. Professionals say that the secret is really in the blending: You want to keep makeup looking natural and fresh. The most unattractive thing is wearing too much, or applying it poorly. Use a well-lit mirror, or you could come up with some pretty scary results.

good grooming

Paying attention to eyebrows, nails, and hairy legs!

Dressing up for your big night marks a kind of coming-of-age for many girls: Finally, it's time to see yourself as the beautiful young lady you really are – or have the potential to be. Grooming rituals can be a bit of pain, or they can be lots of fun, depending on your attitude. Since you're obligated to keep yourself well groomed in order to look your best, you might as well adopt a positive attitude, and have fun with all the fussing necessary to become the best "you" possible.

If you've never shaped your *eyebrows* before, now might be a good time. But once again, I urge you to do your plucking well in advance of your big night, in case your skin is sensitive and goes a little red. Really, your best bet would be to have a professional do your brows as it can be very tricky to shape

them just right. Your mother, aunt, or older sister might also be able to help. But if you do decide to pluck them yourself, make sure you don't remove too much hair. It's much better to have brows that are a little thicker than ones that are too thin. After all, they might not grow back, and you'll be forced to pencil them in for life!

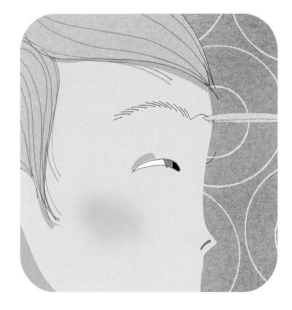

regularly "clean up" your brows with some slight plucking.

If you have other facial hair that's been bugging you, especially the common "mustache," don't despair: There are easy ways of dealing with this. The small wax strips that are available at drugstores are quite efficient. But again, use them at least a couple of days before your big night, in case there's any redness. Follow the instructions on the package carefully, and remember to always "test" a bit of the product on yourself first. Some girls choose to

bleach the hair on their upper lips. There are gentle bleaches available precisely for this purpose, but be extremely careful when following the directions, and always do a small patch test on your arm first.

In terms of *hairy legs*, it's totally your call. If your hair is rather light and

Your eyebrows are supposed to start directly above the inner corners of your eyes. The point of the eyebrow that's highest should be slightly beyond the outer corner of your iris and should taper off to the end. Again, having a professional wax your brows for the first time would give you a proper guideline to follow. Then you can

you do get used to it after a while, and eventually, only a limited amount of hair grows back. It is quite expensive though, so it might be well beyond your budget. There are also other techniques for removing hair, such as sugaring. But again, done professionally, this can be expensive. There are affordable waxing strips and kits available at drugstores that may be a little awkward to use initially, but work quite well.

You might want to get a friend to help you if you decide to attempt waxing yourself. It's much easier when you have an extra pair of hands. Of course, you can always resort to old-fashioned shaving, but make sure your mom is okay with it. Besides the nicks and cuts you might endure before you get the knack of handling a razor, once you start shaving, there may be no turning back – the hair will often come in stubbly and unsightly. Don't you just *love* being a girl?!

sparse (lucky you!), you may choose to do nothing at all. Waxing is always a better option than shaving, or using depilatories. With waxing, the hair doesn't grow back as heavily, and doesn't get as stubbly. Of course, professional waxing is best, although it can be painful at first. Be rest assured,

Now for *the nails*: There seems to have been a real nail-polish explosion these last few years, with the most wonderful colors available, and nail-art becoming more and more popular. Nicely groomed nails are mandatory if you're going after

63

Dear Jeanne:
I really want to wear black to my graduation party, but my parents think it looks too "Goth." What's your opinion?

Emily

A

Dear Emily:
An all black look does make quite the dramatic statement, and I can see why your parents think it looks "Goth," even though that might not be your intention. I love wearing black myself, but it might be a good idea to break some of that black up by injecting a fabulous bright color, like hot pink, or lime green. Red and black are also very cool. And white and black look really elegant together. Again, I adore black, but just make sure you don't overdose on it.

an expert to take care of all the filing, cuticle trimming, and polishing. If not, you can practice giving yourself a good manicure, or get a friend to give you one, and then return the favor!

First, soak your fingernails in warm soapy water for a few minutes. Then, take an orange stick (these are wooden sticks available at a drugstore) and use the pointed end to clean beneath the surface of the nail (but don't dig too deeply, or you'll create pockets that could invite dirt and infection). Then, use the flat end of the stick to gently push your cuticles back. This is a much better approach than cutting your cuticles, because once you do, they'll grow back with a vengeance. Then, take an emery board, and file your nails to your desired shape. Oval is always flattering, and won't "shorten" your fingers the way a squared-off shape might, but it really is personal preference. Once your nails are looking good, massage your hands with a nice hand lotion. Rinse the surface of your nails with water, and towel them dry. Now you're

a total, well-groomed look, but that doesn't mean they necessarily have to be polished. You might just want to have them buffed. If you are going to splurge and treat yourself to a professional manicure for your big night, you'll have

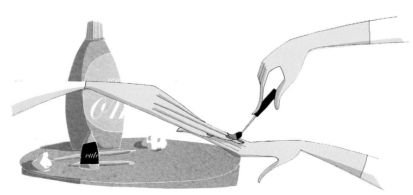

ready for polish. It's always good to use a clear base-coat: It protects the surface of your nail, and helps the polish adhere. Allow the base-coat to dry, and then apply one or two coats of color. You can use an orange stick to trace around the cuticle beds to remove any excess polish. Finally, it's a good idea to use a topcoat, once you've given your nails a chance to dry. A topcoat will protect the polish, and help keep it from chipping. Please have patience when it comes to drying your nails. A good fifteen minutes is mandatory to let the polish set. Otherwise, you'll just muck up your nails and be frustrated.

Since good grooming – and looking good – is a head-to-toe effort, you may also want a pedicure, especially if you're wearing open-toed shoes. Again, a professional pedicure is quite the luxury,

but if you can't afford one, just follow the basic procedures of a manicure, but on your feet instead. The only thing you'll want to add is a good scrubbing with a "foot file" or pumice stone (something that removes the dry, dead skin on your heels and the bottoms of your feet). Always "file" your feet after they've been soaked, so that the skin is softened. And indulge in the luxury of a foot massage – few things are as relaxing! Find a friend whose feet you can massage, and vice versa. Before polishing your toes, you might want to use "toe-separators" (pieces of foam or cardboard that keep your toes apart for easier polish application). If you don't have any "toe-separators," just use pieces of tissue, woven in and out of your toes, to keep them apart. Once again, after applying your polish and topcoat, give your toes a chance to dry properly. Spending the rest of the day in open-toed shoes is best.

the ritual of getting ready

The art of preparation, and the fun of doing a dry run . . .

There's an old saying: "Life is a journey, not a destination." You could say the same about the dress-up experience for your big night out. Ultimately, the greatest joy lies in the preparation, not in merely looking at the final outcome – as stunning as you're bound to be!

Getting ready can be a very personal ritual, or you might be the kind of person who enjoys the company of others at such an exciting time. Many girls love getting ready with their friends. You could even have a "dry run" or "dress rehearsal" for your big night prep. Ideally, a pajama party could be great fun, and give you the chance to exchange ideas for your big night transformation. You could also practice your dance steps, talk about your hopes and fantasies for your big night, and make firm plans about everything from transportation to exactly where to get ready.

Your sleepover could be like a mini spa night, where you and your friends give yourselves manicures and pedicures, experiment with facials, pluck eyebrows, wax legs, try on your outfits, play around with accessories, and work on perfecting your makeup and hairstyle.

If you decide to give yourselves facials, there are lots of commercial

"It's fun to put on nice clothes and straighten your hair and do face masks and . . . makeup, and it makes you feel like a princess."

MAYA, AGE 14

products around on drugstore shelves. Just make sure that you give yourself a "patch" test on the inside of your forearm with any new products you want to use on your face. It's best to wait twenty-four hours to see if you have an allergic reaction to these products. But there are also a wide variety of facial recipes that you can concoct yourself using household ingredients. Here's one recipe I came across for an avocado facial:

The Avocado Facial

Avocados are rich in vitamins A, B, D, E, and lecithin. Avocados leave skin soft and smooth. Avocado pulp is rich and nourishing – great for dry skin. Make sure the avocados you use are not overripe. Put a little mashed avocado on your wrist. Leave awhile. Wash off. Wait twenty-four hours. If your skin is irritated by it, skip this facial. If you are allergic to any of the ingredients in the facial, skip the steps that use these ingredients.

BEFORE YOU START

1. Wash your hands with soap and water.

2. Wash all the bowls, spoons, cups, whisk, and any other utensils you will be using with soap and water. Sterilize these with boiling water. (Note: Do not boil glass items as these can crack and injure you. Certain plastics can melt.) Make sure all surfaces you use for preparing this facial are clean. Remember: For home facials, hygiene and cleanliness are all important.

3. Cut open an avocado. Put the seed with a little pulp in one bowl, the rest of the pulp in another bowl.

4. Put some fresh rose petals into a separate bowl.

5. Fill a kettle with water and set that to boil.

6. Wear a hair band or shower cap to keep your hair off your face.

7. Collect some cotton pads, a clean towel, and one tablespoon of milk.

8. Soak two sterile cotton pads with rose water.

Now you are ready for your facial.

THE FACIAL

1. Dip a pair of clean cotton pads into the milk. Use these pads to wipe your makeup off. Discard leftover milk.

2. Wash off the milk with lots of water.

3. Gently rub your face with a little avocado pulp and almond flour.

4. Wash them off with lots of water.

5. Dry your face with a clean towel.

6. Pour boiling water into the bowl of rose petals.

7. With the towel forming a "tent" over your head and the bowl, keep your face about 20 cm above the bowl. (Caution: Skip this step if you are an asthmatic. The steam could trigger an attack. Skip this step if you have thread veins. The heat could worsen your condition.)

8. Relax and let the steam cleanse your face for ten minutes.

9. Mash the rest of the avocado pulp. Apply it as a face pack.

10. Place a cotton pad soaked with rose water on each eye.

11. Relax and leave them on for ten minutes. Remove.

12. Wash off the face pack with lots of water.

13. Dip two new cotton pads in rose water to tone and cleanse your face further.

14. Apply your favorite moisturizer.

(The above recipe is based on one taken from *www.womanht.com*)

• • • • • •

You can also get creative and make up your own recipes for facials as long as you test the ingredients on your arm first. To remove dark circles, you might try placing slices of cucumber over your eyes, or apply wet teabags to reduce

69

Dear Jeanne:
I want to wear a miniskirt to our big family reunion bash, but my mother thinks it's too short. How short is too short?

Leggy

Dear Leggy:
While microminis have definitely had their moments in fashion, they don't suit everybody. If you feel a mini is the way to go, make sure you don't feel too self-conscious about how short it really is. Wearing an ultra-short skirt with colorful, opaque tights is your best bet, and will certainly ease any feeling of discomfort. You might also want to wear your mini with a fab pair of satin pants underneath. That layered look is very hip and happening. The bottom line is this: If it doesn't feel good, don't wear it!

brushes, rollers, curling and straightening irons, and any other beauty products they might want to share. The more options you have, the more things you can try, and the closer you'll likely get to the look you're after. It's also great to turn your friends on to fabulous products that you've discovered, and you never know what interesting things you might get introduced to.

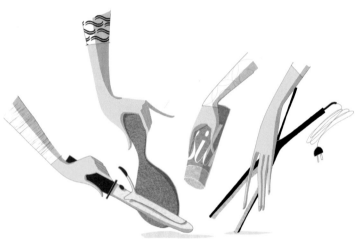

puffiness. I hated my freckles when I was young, and heard that lemon juice can help "bleach them out." I rubbed my face with a half-lemon night after night, but my freckles never did go away. A couple of years later, freckles were considered very "in" and we all started painting fake freckles on our faces! Nowadays, freckles are considered quite cool.

In order to make the most of your hair and makeup "trials," ask everyone to bring all their cosmetics, makeup

Because seeing is believing, it would be a good idea to have a digital or Polaroid camera handy. That way you can take shots of one another, and check them out to see how you look once you're all dressed up. A photo can also help you decide which outfit, or which accessories, look best. But don't ever think you look fat in a photo! Remember, photographs automatically put ten pounds on you, so you might not look as svelte as you'd hoped. Just blame it on the photo. I always do!

When the big day finally arrives, you'll want to take as much time as

try dimming the bathroom lights, and lighting a couple of candles. Your favorite soft music playing in the background will add to the relaxing atmosphere. This is your own precious time to dream about the big fancy adventure in store, and to really feel good about yourself. You've arrived, darling! Luxuriate in that knowledge.

possible for your actual preparation. Even though you'll be tremendously excited, and maybe even a little nervous, make sure you eat something, so you don't start feeling faint, or worse, grumpy. If you can do some exercise that day, or even some yoga, that would really help relax you. For the ultimate relaxation luxury, though, take a good old-fashioned bubble bath. Have a little moisturizer in the water, too, just so your skin feels silky smooth. You might

big night out checklist

Every little thing to keep in mind . . .

Leading up to your big night, there are several things to think about beyond what you'll be wearing. And while these things don't have that much to do with "fashion," they all have to do with "style."

1. How are you going to get to the event? Even Cinderella had to think about her coach. If a parent will drive you, and pick you up, that's great. But you might have to take a taxi, or even public transportation. If that's the case, try to arrange going with a friend, or a group. Then again, if it's a group, remember that taxis won't usually accommodate more than four people. If there's a large group going, you might consider taking a limousine – quite the splurge, but oh-so-divine, and an adventure you'll never forget. But since that option is so pricey, and fairy godmothers are few and far between, it's a luxury you might only be able to fantasize about for now.

2. What will your curfew be? While it might be fun to stay out all night, reality has a funny way of creeping up on us: Make sure discussions with your parents about your curfew start well in advance of your big night. It may be a good idea to find out what some of your friends' curfews are, just to give you and your parents a

Dear Jeanne:
Should my toe polish match my nail polish? And should that all match my lipstick?

Matchy Matchy

Dear Matchy:
There are no rules about this kind of thing. But I do prefer it when lips and nails match. Still, you might be going for white, or blue, or green nail polish. And I certainly wouldn't advise putting those colors on your lips! As for toes, they definitely don't have to match your nails. I usually prefer natural-looking nails, with a stronger color for the toes. But that's just my personal preference.

frame of reference. Your negotiating skills certainly come into play here. You'll have to display an extreme amount of responsibility to your parents in the weeks leading up to your big night. But, ultimately, you'll have to respect the restraints they feel they have to place on you. Remember, nothing lasts forever. As good a time as you're bound to have, you have to be mature enough to realize that all good things eventually come to an end, and sometimes, too much of a good thing can turn bad. It's better to leave a great party on a high note.

You might want to have a sleepover with some friends. Make these arrangements in advance, so you don't find yourself on the phone in the middle of your fantastic evening, desperately pleading with your parents to either let you have friends over, or let you sleep out.

If you do plan on getting your hair done professionally, or getting a manicure or pedicure, make sure you've budgeted properly. Besides the salon rate, you'll also want to give your hairdresser or manicurist a 10% to 15% tip. And you'll want to give the person washing your hair a small tip as well – say, around $2.00. If you're old enough to be going to a salon for these services, you're old enough to courteously tip! Make sure that you book all your appointments well in

advance. And, in terms of time, while it's best to get your hair done as late in the day as possible so that it doesn't start falling down or going limp, make sure you get home at least an hour ahead of when you need to leave for your big night. Being stressed and rushing are the last things you'd want to deal with. Remember to wear a shirt that buttons down the front when you go for your hair appointment, so you won't ruin your hairdo when you change.

While some may feel that corsages are old-fashioned, many girls still love the romance of a corsage, especially for a formal prom. If you have a date, he should be aware that it is customary to give the girl a corsage. And wrist corsages are certainly the most popular and easy to wear. But if you're worried that your date might not come through, you can open a discussion about prom flowers by asking him if he has a preference for his boutonniere because you want to get

75

"I'm gonna dress what's me. I'm gonna act what's me. And I'm gonna sing what's me."

Q

Dear Jeanne:
I don't think I'd ever be able to afford the kind of dress I'm really longing for. I heard about places that rent formal gowns. Do you think this would be a good idea for me?

Borrowing Betsy

A

Dear Betsy:
While it's true that you might be able to rent some fantastic creation for a fraction of the price the dress would normally cost, you really have think long and hard about this. Renting a gown won't be all that cheap and do you really want to wear your fantasy dress once and once only? While buying an expensive dress is way too extravagant for most young people, renting one could be just as extravagant. Try using your creative imagination and see if there's some kind of interesting alternative you could come up with for your big night out that won't break the bank.

him one, and you think it would be cool to wear matching flowers. You'll know soon enough whether this guy is planning on giving you a corsage! If he's not because, perhaps, he can't afford one, don't despair. If you have your heart set on donning flowers on your big night, why not just order your own little flowers and wear them in your hair, or pinned onto your evening bag.

● ● ● ● ● ●

Okay. . . . The big day has arrived: It's time to put all your dreams and fantasy into play!

In the morning, get all your things together: your dress or outfit, lingerie, shoes, and all your accessories. Put them together in one place so you won't be freaking out at the last minute, looking for stray stuff.

Take a shower early in the day, and have your manicure and pedicure done so that your nails have plenty of time to dry. Toenails take especially long.

If you're doing your hair yourself, start a couple of hours before it's time to go, just to get it right. You could start your makeup about an hour before, but this doesn't mean you should be applying a lot! If you're opting for the ultra-minimal approach, like gloss and eye shadow, you won't need as long, but don't forget to moisturize your face, hands, and entire body. And if you're using perfume, remember that a very little goes a long way.

Wait until the end to get dressed. After all, you don't want to run your stockings or wrinkle your dress.

Make sure you have everything you need in your evening bag, from money for a phone call (since you might not want to take your cell phone), money for a taxi if you're going by cab, and any ticket you might need, to your lipstick, a mirror, a comb, perhaps breath mints, and your key.

Allow enough time for a few pictures. There's no doubt that you'll want a precious record of the new and improved gorgeous you. You're creating memories that will last

Q

Dear Jeanne:
I'm worried about the straps of my vintage dress slipping down. How can I make sure this doesn't happen?
Oops

A

Dear Oops:
Even J. Lo had a problem keeping her slinky Versace dress up at an awards show a few years back – and that's a common problem. The solution is using two-sided sticky tape. Just put it on your body first, and then press the fabric of your dress to it.

a lifetime. And take the time to admire your beautiful self in the mirror before you step out: You are a true original, a glorious work of art – exquisite on the inside as well as out. The world's a pretty fabulous place, and it's time for you to make your glamorous mark. Don't compare yourself to anyone: You are wonderfully unique. Tonight, relish your independence and that special style dream you managed to bring to life. It's time to shine, sweetie! This night will stay with you forever: your first, fancy, big night out. It's bound to be magical. Have an amazing time!